C000173016

ON OBSESSION

Malcolm Knox

MELBOURNE
UNIVERSITY
PRESS

MELBOURNE UNIVERSITY PRESS
An imprint of Melbourne University Publishing Limited
187 Grattan Street, Carlton, Victoria 3053, Australia
mup-info@unimelb.edu.au
www.mup.com.au

First published 2008
Text © Malcolm Knox, 2008
Design and typography © Melbourne University Publishing Ltd 2008

Text design by Alice Graphics
Cover design by Nada Backovic Designs
Typeset by TypeSkill
Printed in Australia by Griffin Press, SA

National Library of Australia Cataloguing-in-Publication entry

Knox, Malcolm, 1966–
On obsession / Malcolm Knox.

9780522855630 (hbk.)

Compulsive behavior.
Obsessive-compulsive disorder

616.8584

Human relationships are as vast as deserts; they demand all daring.
Patrick White, *Voss*

I

When my maternal grandfather died, he left his secrets in a Highland Citrus fruit carton on the top shelf of his wardrobe.

Roy died in 1995, at eighty-seven. My elder brother and I were his only grandchildren, and he'd always insisted that we call him Roy—no Grandpa or Pop, just Roy. When we referred to 'Gran and Roy', listeners would assume he was our gran's boyfriend.

Roy was a witty, placid kind of man, a sportsman and a gardener, who never lost his heroic status in our eyes. His father had been shot near Villers-Bretonneux in 1918 and Roy, still a child but the eldest of three, had to raise his family. He became a medical technician although, if his father had survived, he might have gone to university and become a doctor. But I wouldn't overstate the multiplier-effect of the war on our family: it's hard to imagine Roy being more respectable or content than he was.

But Roy held a secret. For seven decades he kept a daily diary. While he was alive I was unaware of its existence, let alone its contents. He guarded his diary with an uncharacteristic zeal. He was married to

Gran for nearly sixty years but never let her see it.

There was a new pocket-sized diary each year, and they were valuable enough for him to keep them all. When he died, Gran let me take the little Highland Citrus carton. I don't think she ever looked inside.

They lay in the box, a motley of leathers and vinyls and marbled cardboards and fake crocodile skins, red and black and green and brown and olive and blue, pregnant with Roy's inner life. If I felt a hesitation over invading my grandfather's privacy, or feared what I might uncover, it was burnt off by the fire of my curiosity.

There were some notepads from the mid 1920s but it was in January 1929, a month before Roy's twenty-first birthday, that the diary became continuous. That week, Bradman scored 112 against England, Sydney had its hottest day for thirty-three years, and there was a Spanish training ship in Sydney Harbour; Roy had a haircut and wrote a letter, played three rounds of golf and saw three films. His mother got out of bed after four days with pleurisy.

I can tell you the temperature, rainfall and humidity of every day that week, and the next, and every day of every week from 1929 to 1993. I can tell you every golf score my grandfather recorded and every movie and musical he saw, until the early 1990s, when the diary shrank down to its essentials: the humidity, the temperature and the rainfall. But it was always brief and to the point. Occasionally he had such a good day that he would effuse: 'Good day'.

Roy loved to tease and he loved practical jokes, and at first I believed his diaries were a joke played on us. But there had to be more than this—why else would he guard them so strictly?

I went for the key dates. He married my grandmother on 26 December 1935: '83 [he always recorded the temperature in Fahrenheit]. Warm + humid + rain at night. Went to Hotel Sydney with Chip [his brother]. Luggage. Married Lillian [*sic*] Ellen at 7PM at St Thomas' Church N. Sydney. To Hotel Sydney later'. The first day of married life? 'Cool day. Left Sydney at 9.50AM with Mrs R. Walker for Bundanoon. Arrived 2PM. Went for walk with Lily. Played deck quoits. 110 people at Royal Hotel.' And the next day: 'Cool weather. Played golf with Lily. 37-36-73. Lily 121. Met Mr & Mrs Russell McNamara. Went to pictures with them at night'. I turned to Sunday 6 April 1941, the date of my mother's birth:

> 65 [Fahrenheit], 59 [per cent humidity]. Some light showers late. Strong S. breeze all day. Took Lily to Strathallen Hospital 7AM + at 11AM she gave birth to a baby daughter Kay. 8lb 6oz. Both well. Brought Jasper [the dog] to Dot + Harley [the neighbours]. They took him to Turramurra.

Perhaps he was loosened up by an even prouder day—the birth of his second grandson, Wednesday 5 October 1966: '60, 50. Cool + cloudy. Kay's second son born at 1am. Malcolm Ross. 8lb 6oz. Darker than Stuart [my elder brother]. Both well. Went to DY [Roy's work]. Not busy. Went to see Kay + baby at night … Coldest Oct for 10 years'. The diaries continue in this vein until 1993, when Roy began to suffer from his first and last chronic illness, lung cancer. The 1993 diary stutters along, its frequency dropping. The final entry, on 31 December, is: '912mm Jan-Dec (36 inches) Normal av. 48 inches'.

This apparent emotional aridity was not unusual for his era. The war diaries of Lyall Howard, the grandfather of the former prime minister, as reproduced in Les Carlyon's *The Great War*, are as cursory as Roy's.[1] Yet there was more in here than the laconic feeling-tone of another era. Roy had maintained this diary every day for sixty-four years; he had hidden it like a criminal burying his past. Clearly there was something hiding behind the weather records and golf scores. Those numbers, available through public records yet written exclusively for himself, must have contained a type of allusive private code. In *Regeneration* Pat Barker writes of Siegfried Sassoon's similarly unenlightening hunting diaries:

> On and on. A terribly meaningless little set of squiggles it would have seemed to anybody else, but for him it had contained the Sussex lanes, the mists, the drizzle, the baying of hounds, clods

flying from under the horses' feet, stag-
gering into the house, bones aching,
reliving the hunt over dinner, and then,
after dinner, shadows on the wall of the
old nursery and Gordon's face in the
firelight, the scent of logs, the warmth,
his whole face feeling numbed and swol-
len in the heat.[2]

There must have been smells, sounds and
sights, memories which those compressed
numbers unlocked for Roy and nobody
else. The ciphers of daily temperature
figures must have encoded a life to which
he alone was privy.

If the daily weather was his portal
into his life's experience, what did the
weather mean to him? What was so important about it that it had to be preserved?

Weather is a grand and open-ended subject to be fixated upon, but then again, as Mark Twain said, everyone complains about the weather but nobody does anything about it. I don't remember Roy talking much about the weather other than to slander the television forecasters. At home he tended to hover around his wall thermometer, but his study didn't accumulate into a body of knowledge that he might pass on like a tribal elder. The only weather advice I remember coming from Roy was that you need wind of 30 knots to bring up whitecaps (which is not, I believe, quite true), and if the barometer is dropping then there is probably rain on the way.

He did love rain, and often predicted it. For him this was a show of optimism, a forecast to brighten, so to speak, the day. Everyone else groaned and rolled their eyes, accusing Roy of being an 'Uncle Alf', referring to an obscure ancestor whose one legacy was a notoriety for predicting rain, and who appeared in the family mythology at no other times. Yet, as I well knew, when you are truly fixated on some object you will find any excuse to bring their name into unrelated conversations whether your listeners know her or not, and at least as far as the weather was concerned, Roy was not that far gone. It was more of a hobby than a constant preoccupation. Or so I had thought.

When Roy died I was nearly thirty years old. I chewed over his diaries for months, going back to them and rereading the entries on the significant days, or picking a day at random to see if I could catch something by surprise. They were clearly a disguise, but for what?

Perhaps the answer lay in plain view. Every day, from 1 January 1929 to early 1993, he kept it going. He started at twenty and didn't stop until he was getting ready to die. I wonder if, at twenty, he saw what an unfinishable lifetime task he was setting himself. I thought back to how I had been at twenty. Perhaps this wasn't a matter of my interrogating Roy's diary, but rather the reverse: the diary was asking questions of me. And this was how it struck me, the essence of the thing that made Roy's diary both necessary and secret.

II

I had always been what we would call a 'focused' kind of child. My childhood was a string of enthusiasms, the most enduring of which was books. I took books everywhere. When we went on family fishing expeditions I was notorious for sulkily dangling a line until the first fish was caught (worth a 20-cent prize from Gran), then packing it up and sitting silently, in the putt-putt boat with five other people, my nose plunged into a novel for the next eight or nine hours.

None of this appeared pathological or unhealthy, and indeed it was encouraged at home and at school. My brother had a more restless nature, and my trance-like powers of concentration were applauded, judged to be a more reliable predictor of success in life.

My reading regime was conducted along Presbyterian lines of Thoroughness First. If I liked one Agatha Christie I would not rest until I had read every Agatha Christie. Novel series were made for readers like me: Arthur Ransome's Swallows and Amazons, Franklin W Dixon's Hardy Boys, Alfred Hitchcock's Three Investigators. Into adolescence it was in for a penny, in for a pound: every James Clavell, every James Michener, every Leon Uris. With the bad ones, I just had to knuckle down harder. In school curricula I approached English texts methodically, slicing up Jane Austen with the skills of both the Iron Chef and the pathological gambler (what are the odds on my needing the brisket, say, to answer an essay question?): a method, I hoped, in my madness. Again, all this was seen and assessed by my educators, not as a sign of mental instability but of great talent and application.

I should have noticed that something was amiss, however, when at eighteen I resolved to read everything.

Not *everything* everything, of course. A crude calculus of shelf space, reading speed and life expectancy cautioned me to trim poetry, plays and most non-fiction from my project. I would read only all the significant novels ever written. With this drawing up of sensible boundaries I could assure myself, if no-one else, that I hadn't broken completely from my moorings.

So: only all the significant novels ever written.

The impetus for this project was that, at around the same age as Roy had started writing his diary, I had just discovered a real book: the book that transforms your eyes, shows you what all the fuss is about. Stendhal's *The Scarlet and the Black* hit me with the force of a conspiracy: Julien Sorel's coming of age in post-Napoleonic France showed me more that was beautiful and wise and (the post-adolescent's Holy Grail) *relevant to my life* than anything else I had read. Why hadn't anybody told me about this? How much more had they been hiding?

Considerably more, it turned out, as I began compiling lists. First I procured the readings from the French, German, Russian and English departments at Sydney University, then took my notepad around bookstores and jotted the names of necessary-seeming authors. Then I copied out a catalogue of Penguin classics and modern classics. If I read all of them, that would be a start.

Although I was enrolled in the university, this work, my real work, was a passion I attacked with the autodidact's enthusiasm and patchiness. Just as Roy had never wanted to train as a meteorologist, I dedicated myself with the purity of the amateur. Not for a second did I question what I was doing. What grander journey to lose myself in? Nobody around me read these books. I sensed that I emanated from a culture of skilled-up barbarians who knew a great deal about material specifics yet nothing about the larger truth I had stumbled upon. How could anyone not have read *The Scarlet and the Black* and be fully alive?

My mission, chosen so enthusiastically and heedless of consequence, entailed as much hardship as exhilaration. The joy came in discovering the Germans, the Russians, the French. The hardship came in having placed Samuel Butler's *The Way of All Flesh*, say, or most of DH Lawrence on the same pedestal, requiring the same devotion of hours, as Tolstoy or Thomas Mann. My naivety about 'significance' led me into whole libraries of dross, but I gritted my teeth and mowed them down. At least they made the blissful discoveries feel both hard-earnt and revealed, singularly, to me.

No doubt I was, psychologically speaking, a few books short of the full library. But I was still years from suspecting this when I came across the mirror to my soul, the writer who surpassed all, the one for whom I would renounce all others.

I'd come across the name Marcel Proust in *The Book of Lists*, of which I was an avid reader in my early teens.[3] Proust's *In Search of Lost Time* was listed in both the ten greatest and ten most boring books ever written. (I think *Moby-Dick* and *Don Quixote*, whose authors and heroes share Proust's intoxicating single-mindedness, were likewise distinguished.) I had no idea that being a Proust-reader, far more than being, say, a *Penthouse*-reader, was tantamount to declaring oneself a wanker. In my history course at Sydney University, I was encouraged to write an essay about Proust's treatment of the Dreyfus affair, which I soon learnt would be as blinkered as going to the Sydney Opera House and seeking its architectural codes in the bathrooms or the under-ground carpark.

With a young man's relentless naivety,
I set about all seven volumes. *Swann's
Way* opened a vein that no history essay
could stanch; the effort it demanded to
slow down and recalibrate attention to the
tortuous winding of those sentences, pen-
dulous with clauses like fruit-heavy trees,
was a form of mental training. Proust's
novel goes on for more than 3000 dense
pages; every now and then a sentence
ends, and another begins, but those sentences are held together by a logic that
demands an unfamiliar, avid, strenuous
kind of reading.

Even though knowing about (if not
reading) Proust has been made fashion-
able, almost a cliché, these days, it would
be truly wankerish to presume knowledge

of his book. So, to condense the uncondensable: the story is narrated by a Parisian looking back on his life in the years before and during World War I. Its enduring philosophical content has to do with the subjective nature of time and the power of sense impressions to unlock memory, such as the madeleine dipped in tea that brings his childhood to life. The story cycles through a series of love affairs that elaborate and recapitulate each other, starting before the narrator's birth, in the love of Charles Swann, a family friend, for a former courtesan, Odette de Crecy. The second love story is the narrator's teenage love for Gilberte, the daughter of Swann and Odette. The third is that of the narrator's aristocrat friend Robert de Saint-

Loup for a prostitute-actress nicknamed Rachel. The fourth is the narrator's love for a duchess, Oriane de Guermantes. The fifth is the secret love that Mme de Guermantes' brother-in-law, the Baron de Charlus, has for young men in general and particularly a violinist named Morel. And building throughout is the narrator's terminal love for a young middle-class woman called Albertine Simonet. The narrator is usually equated with Proust himself, as they were both young bourgeois who ascended to high society during the belle epoque, but there are significant differences, not least that Proust was attracted to men.

While the seven volumes portray the zenith and slow death of the belle epoque, and many other events of interest (including the Dreyfus affair!) in a social comedy of successive set-pieces, the essential subject matter is love, particularly obsessive love. All the loves work off the template of Swann's for Odette. Even though she is not 'his type', Swann becomes maddened by the need to possess her. Odette has no particular qualities, and loving her ensures Swann's social downfall, but it is her very undesirability that makes Swann's obsession both a puzzle and a solution, because, as he grows morbidly jealous, trapped in his own theories and counter-theories, Swann is demonstrating what Proust believes underpins this most powerful kind of love. Love is a temporary random alignment of forces within the lover, and the beloved is the accidental person who steps into the vacuum that these forces create at a particular moment. Once there, she is fixed: 'When we are in love with a woman, all we are doing is projecting on to her a state of our own self; consequently what is important is not the merit of the woman, but the intensity of that state ... '[4]

Swann's Way, setting up 2500 pages of unhappy love, changed me. From a distance of a century, and half a world, I had found someone who knew my private self, that part of me which I kept hidden.

III

It had taken only one girl to show me the difference between obsession and its neighbouring echoes. I was sixteen, on the phone with my friend J, a girl we knew called Heidi and her friend Sandra. In sparkling form, as I often would be with a girl who couldn't see me, I struck up a rapport with Sandy and, before I knew what I was doing, invited her to a school musical.

What I had not accounted for were the three or four days between the phone call and my first date. By that time I was sunk— not by an image, as I hadn't seen Sandra yet, but by the words of our phone conversation, which replayed on an endless loop; the words I would say to her when we met; the words I used to caution myself against saying the wrong words. Very often it was only one word: *Sandra, Sandra, Sandra, Sandra.* I did not know her, but during those few days she flooded my consciousness. *Sandra, Sandra, Sandra.* The torment of not thinking about her was salved only by the torment of thinking about her. I was as mad as a blowfly trapped between two panes.

When the night arrived, having gone through every conceivable flow-chart of 'if this, then that', stocked up on memorised witticisms and conversation topics, mentally rehearsed every eventuality except how I would greet her, I panicked. The moment I saw her I lunged forth with a slobbering pucker. I don't remember much about the night, but I do remember Sandra's grunt of surprise as she realised I was coming at her—the type of grunt the driver of a car must make when she realises the oncoming semitrailer is not going to miss.

Strangely, although I had an eidetic recall of every word, pause, giggle and intake of breath from our phone conversation, I would retain nothing of the date itself except the monstrousness of my greeting. I couldn't sleep that night, of course, for the resumption of the electric humming: *Sandra, Sandra, Sandra, Sandra.* The date had been a kind of holiday from this. The only time I was not obsessed with Sandra, not even thinking about her, had been while I was with her.

The next day in class, when J asked me how it had gone, I smirked that it had gone very well indeed. He asked me what Sandra's breasts were like. I grinned with the knowingness of all boys who know nothing and said, 'Mangoes'.

Mangoes? I had been too scared to let my eyes drop beneath her fringe, let alone qualify myself as a fruiterer of the female form.

'Ah', J said appreciatively. 'Mangoes.'

For a few days we included a mango reference in every conversation, and I became fixated on the word mango. But events moved too fast for me: there was a party the following weekend, I wasn't there, and Sandra was officially going out with J, whose many advantages over me included his gift for not thinking about her at all.

It turned out that everybody called her Sandy, not Sandra, a depletion of the magic of names which helped me get over her. I never saw much of Sandy after that (J dumped her), but clearly I have not forgotten. A quarter of a century later, if she failed to remember the event, or me, at all, that would be a relief amounting to forgiveness. Nevertheless, if I ran into her today my knees would turn, like Humbert Humbert's at the first sight of Lolita, into the reflections of knees in rippling water.[5]

Sandra's incompatibility fitted the slot of, and formed the pattern for, my obsessions: blithe girls, indifferent to my subtle charms, noisy and vivacious and full of themselves, promiscuous with others if not me, boisterous good-timers who, if I ever let slip that I was in love with them, would tear me to shreds with their pitying generous laughter. But I could not let it slip, because the way I loved was more an incurable illness than a feeling for another person. What girl would not run for her life if you told her you woke up imagining conversations with her, you silently narrated to her your smallest domestic or daily acts, you composed endless letters to her, you were ferociously inquisitive about everything she was doing in the menacing blank sheet of her unknown days? What happy, sociable girl would not have the instinct to sense danger?

For me it was difficult too, but thanks to Proust I had a framework for what was happening to me—if not an escape hatch then a consoling voice telling me that I was not alone: 'Few people understand either the purely subjective nature of the phenomenon of love, or how it creates a supplementary person who is quite different from the one who bears our beloved's name in the outside world, and is mostly formed from elements within ourselves'.[6] A hundred years earlier an asthmatic Frenchman, different from me in innumerable respects, had loved in the same way as I:

> Every day since I had first seen Albertine, I had entertained thousands of thoughts about her, I had carried on, with what I called 'her', an extended interior conversation, in which I had questions put to her and had her answer them, think and act ... This Albertine was little more than an outline: everything else that had been added to her was of my own making, for our own contribution to our love ... is greater than that of the person we love.[7]

Yes!—I mean, *Yes!*

He consoled me for falling in love with women who could never make me happy and whom I didn't even like. It was not a burden I had to carry alone. If nobody understood my pain, then I had a friend in Charles Swann. The Duchesse de Guermantes tells Swann that it's absurd to be in love with someone so unworthy of him

> with the wisdom of people not in love who believe a man of sense should be unhappy only over a person who is worth it; which is rather like being surprised that anyone should condescend to suffer from cholera because of so small a creature as the comma bacillus.[8]

Again: *yes!*

I held no illusions about mine being a 'right' or 'healthy' way to love, or one that was going to lead anywhere but back to myself. I knew it was wrong to be so fixated on girls who were not so much real people as a constantly re-forming creation of my loneliness. But against the knowledge of its wrongness was an equally powerful notion of its dignity. As an adolescent emerging into adulthood, you are wandering in a dark forest looking for signposts. In the cultural air, one of those signposts said that obsessive behaviour was not only encouraged but was the sine qua non of getting ahead. I was too much a product of my world not to have learnt that I could not really succeed in anything unless I was devoting every waking and dreaming moment to it. Dare to dream! This was the 1980s, when the idea of competitiveness was shifting into a higher gear, when our great economic fear was of being overrun by a nation whose workers slept on the train to maximise the number of hours they could be in the office. And so, rather than giving me an alternative view, literature was reinforcing the dominant signposts of the culture. When I looked at my heroes in literature, their common essence was their single-mindedness: the great men, the great women, the soldiers, the artists, the lovers, the splendid failures, the figures of genius both on and behind the page, all had this in common. They thought of only one thing, and the

unhappiness this caused was the soil from
which their genius grew.

So it was very confusing indeed.

IV

If increasingly I found my soulmates in fiction, I knew that I was not created in the same way. I was reaching an age where I had ceased resisting the likeness between myself and my parents and started to examine what it was and what it had left me with: to examine Proust's proposition that 'after a certain age, and even if our inner development varies, the more we become ourselves, the more are family characteristics accentuated'.[9]

If gestures, patterns of thought, habits of speech and so on are heritable, it would be anomalous if my temperament in love, disabled by my one-track mind, hadn't shown up in someone before me.

By my twentieth birthday, when I was coming to the end of my first reading of Proust (whose narrator was also uncommonly fascinated by the weather, a legacy inherited from his father), I was gaining glimmers of understanding.[10] I had transformed a succession of girls into mysteries of galactic scope; I had taken on a reading project which had no boundaries and no end. I longed to throw myself into

something that would last a lifetime—
which, in the absence of the spiritual
ambitions that drove my literary heroes,
might have been my atheistic lunge for the
infinite.

It had to have come from somewhere.

In my family, the survival skills have
passed down the female side while the
temperaments have come from the men.
From our grandmothers and our mother,
my brother and I inherited the ability to
get on with people. From our grandfathers
and our father, we inherited the blood.

Roy had the persistence to write down
the weather every day for sixty-four
years. But he was a calm man. The hot-
heads were on the paternal side.

My father, who was an engineer, came from a family distinguished by various public and private achievements and a touch of eccentricity—interesting and highly intelligent people, yet with an undercurrent, like a hot wire buried in otherwise safe circuitry. Had my father suffered the kinds of fixations I'd had? During my teens he undertook a mid-career MBA, and once I came across one of those personal 'self-assessment' questionnaires on which, when it asked for 'personal weaknesses', he wrote something to the effect of 'No confidence around women'. Aha! But I couldn't see him strung to the same wheels of fire as I was. By his mid-twenties he was married, with a profession, a mortgage and two children, and the kind of established place in his world that I could not yet picture for myself.

Still, there was the volatile element. I have strong memories of his being wound tight with urgency, ambitious not so much for the years or the months ahead as for the very minutes in which he was living. He had an excitable temper in certain circumstances which revolved around the completion of a task. He simply could not rest, could not eat, could not return to humanity, until he had done certain things. They were not grand obsessions. Our story involved no Watts Tower, no glass cathedral (but I don't for a minute buy the line that the size and grandeur of an obsession endows it with a certain immunity; saving the world does not redeem a cruel parent). My father, who was not at all cruel to us, would nonetheless fly into rages which were transparently aimed at himself but threw sparks at the bystanders. His rages revolved around finishing the tidying of his workshop, or weeding one of the garden beds, or getting the last leaf out of the pool, or ordering the last page of his stamp collection, before lunch. They were ordinary pursuits. What was not ordinary was that he would sacrifice everyone's happiness and harmony, and at times would have given everything away, *everything*, just so he could complete what he was doing. And then he could relax and be nice again. There was a ferocity in his devotion to the moment that was terrifying for a child, terrifying when I see it in myself, terrifying when I see my children seeing it in me, and terrifying when I see it in my children.

What for Roy was a constant but low-level preoccupation that found its outlet in a few minutes of daily record-keeping was for my father concentrated into tiny bubbles of passion, like a sauce reduced down to an intensity of flavour, unforgivable from the outside because the activities themselves seemed so trivial and so easily postponable. Not for him they weren't. I doubt that even for him the content of these tasks was all-important; more, it was the pressing need to rule a line under one thing before moving on to the next.

He could not keep several balls in the air; his temperament required that he do things sequentially. Long after this, when the therapeutic benefits of 'closure' became widely touted, I would laugh: you didn't have to tell us about the importance of 'closure'!

And so, in these moments, we sat at the table waiting for him in a kind of fear that was more tangible to us than it ever was to him. My mother would make him aware that he was holding us up, and the tug-of-war between our needs and his could sometimes pump an awful surge of pressure into the thin membrane that was his temper. When he blew his top, it demonstrated the law of conservation of energy: that intensity of feeling would depart from him, float across the kitchen and lodge in us. He would be calm, and we would be fuming.

The whole sorry process was something I would inherit. But this is a trait that only paternity can fully bring out, and it was still some years before I had my own family and would see the flow of my father's hot blood into mine, and get an inkling that the infatuations, the lifelong endeavours, the grand obsessions into which I threw myself sprang from fear, and were a buffer between myself and life, a barrier I was setting up between myself and harm's way.

V

Like a steak chef who hates the sight of blood, I use the word 'obsession' with flinching resignation to necessity. The word carries a baggage of Freudian and other technical-psychological specificity that I neither understand nor, in this space, want to explore. Clearly the word is no longer doing what it used to do, when we can commonly hear someone saying they are 'obsessed' with ringtones or are 'obsessing over' their hair extensions. It is not that ringtones and hair extensions may not be the subject of genuine obsession in the right (or wrong) hands; it is that we use the word to describe too many weaker emotions, just as we use 'flu' for a common cold or 'migraine' for a headache. And when a psychiatric term becomes a perfume label, we know our age is administering its last rites.

By the time I was twenty-one, Proust and others had nudged me towards thinking of myself as a writer—as happened to the Queen in Alan Bennett's *The Uncommon Reader*, the novelists inhabiting my head demanded, from me, some randomly jotted responses.[11] I was seeking to articulate the feelings that were overpowering me. It was an involuted desire, but again Proust was giving me licence:

> We may converse our whole life away, without speaking anything other than the interminable repetitions that fill the vacant minute; but the steps of thought which we take during the lonely work of artistic creation all lead us downwards, deeper into ourselves, the only direction which is not closed to us, the only direction in which we can advance, albeit with much greater travail, towards an outcome of truth.[12]

Writing was a way in, but also a way out.

While validating unhappiness as the fertile manure of art, Proust also likened love to disease:

And this disease which was Swann's
love had so proliferated, it was so closely
entangled with all Swann's habits, with
all his actions, with his thoughts, his
health, his sleep, his life, even with what
he wanted after his death, it was now so
much a part of him, that it could not have
been torn from him without destroying
him almost entirely; as they say in surgery, his love was no longer operable.[13]

In the late 1980s and early 1990s it seemed
that feelings were being medicalised. The
world was catching up with Proust. In 1990
I began working as a paralegal for a law
firm which was representing the tobacco
industry in a misleading-advertising case.
(I had a ferocious crush on a woman who

worked there to whom I wrote a letter saying simply: 'I'm the one who keeps looking at you'. To my desperate disappointment and limitless relief, she showed no sign of noticing me at all.) My job was to be a reading monkey, to summarise into predetermined taxonomies medical articles relating to tobacco and health, which the lawyers could then use in examining expert witnesses. A key taxonomic subject was the medical and societal synonym for obsession. I developed a special interest in *addiction*.

Because the worrying kinds of behaviour I'd been discovering in myself had no basis in a physical substance, like a drug, I was drawn to the psychological aspects of addiction. By 1990 these were well established by the *Diagnostic and Statistic Manual of Mental Disorders*, known as the DSM, published by the American Psychiatric Association. I was reading the third version, the DSM-III[14], which listed diagnostic criteria for addiction: a preoccupation with the drug between times of usage; breaking personal resolutions on how much of the drug to use; repeated failures to cut back or stop using it; being intoxicated at inappropriate times; reducing habitual social, recreational or other activities in favour of using the substance; and continued use despite knowing about the problems it has been or will be causing.

I ran this checklist past my history of crushes. Had I been preoccupied with the girl between the times I had managed to see her? Yes, even more than when I had been with her. Had I promised myself not to phone her, or write to her, or scratch her name into my desk, and then broken that promise? Copiously. Had I sworn, after some rejection or epiphany, to stop fixating on her, and then failed? Every firm resolution thus far had been merely the first step in a subsequent backsliding. Had I been obsessively chasing a girl at inappropriate times or at the expense of other activities? Well, once I was so enamoured of a Turkish girl when I was living in London that I told her I was going to cash in my return ticket to Sydney, cancel my plans to backpack in Europe, fly us both to Turkey, reconcile her with her estranged family, get a house in a village, and look after her happily ever after. In these promises I was utterly sincere. Luckily, she rolled her eyes and went her own way. And finally, did I continue falling in love in this way despite knowing how much harm it was doing me? Well, the last time I'd looked at Proust or Garcia Marquez or Mann or Flaubert, being harmed was what was so beautiful about love, and the most unhealthy, the most dangerous, the most addictive form of love—obsessive love—was the highest state to which humanity could aspire.

Was love the problem, then, or was the medicalised idea of addiction not quite apt? With a little imagination, the DSM's criteria of addiction could be applied to shopping, religion, eating, gambling, computer games, dogs, cats ... even smoking. Since the 1980s the idea of the 'addictive personality' has become so commonplace that it is now a standard excuse or reason for renunciation. How many of us repudiate some promised pleasure because we don't trust our own 'addictive personalities'? Thanks to the currency of the 'addictive personality' and the cult of medicalised self-knowledge, never being able to stop is seen as a legitimate health-based reason for never starting.

But just as the recidivist alcoholic is the one who never really wants to give up, I didn't really want to be inoculated against love. Who does? Love, while sharing so much with the other addictions, is unique. Even when it can ruin your life, nobody seriously argues it is a bad thing. Indeed, since the death of God, love has become our deity. To seek a cure for it would be a kind of madness.

The final shortcoming of the addiction model, as a means of understanding my unhappiness, was that addiction and obsession were clearly different. I had been infatuated with people without being at all addicted to their presence. My love for some girls flourished under the condition of never seeing or talking to them. Indeed, I had so little to talk about with one girl, and was so underwhelmed by those conversations we did have, that I deployed every possible excuse to avoid her. In her absence, my love thrived. Conversely, it was evidently easy to be addicted yet not obsessed. Nicotine was a prime example. I doubted many smokers thought about cigarettes obsessively, other than when they were trying to give up. And would heroin be as psychologically addictive without the mind-eating preoccupation with how to score, how to shoot up, how to organise one's life around it? Heroin without those routines is methadone: addiction without obsession.

In a year of turning over every stone in the medical literature of addiction, I found only its inadequacy. Having been drawn by the commonalities between mine and a more general human experience—'I am not alone!'—I was developing a sense of the differences, the uniqueness of my case. 'I am alone!'

At twenty-four I was still fully engaged in my read-everything project but had instituted a rule to read only one book per author (the seven parts of *In Search of Lost Time* counted as one). Thus constrained, I might be able to reach my target by the time I turned seventy-five, providing nobody wrote anything worthwhile after 1990.

When in 1990 I read Proust for a second time, I realised I had forgotten a good deal. I tried to construe this as a virtue, for just as the narrator triumphs over lost time in the little unsolicited moments which bring the past to life, part of the fabric of the book, for narrator and reader alike, is the experience of forgetting. By losing so many events and characters, I was unwittingly creating space for their joyful retrieval later on.

Alternatively, my poor memory might have been a by-product of my reading project, which could seem more dogged than inspired, my life as a reader more like rock-breaking than what Jorge Luis Borges called 'as rich as any other life'.[15] I imagine my face, as I slogged through book six, *The Fugitive* (the nadir of the narrator's descent into obsessive jealousy), looking grim and sweaty as I tried not to ponder how such a pleasure could have turned into such a chore.

But Proust could still provide moments of transcendent joy, and I would discover during this second reading a refinement of a link I had vaguely sensed between fixation and memory. Very early in *Swann's Way* Proust writes of trying to capture and preserve the 'volatile essence' of anticipating a goodnight kiss from his mother, and compares himself with

> those possessed by some mania who do their utmost not to think of anything else while they are shutting a door, so as to be able, when the morbid uncertainty returns to them, to confront it

victoriously with the memory of the
moment when they did shut the door.[16]

He revisits the image, as he revisits most
things, several books later:

> It is as if there arises in us, in relation to
> the phrase and to the exactness of our
> memory, a doubt of the same kind as is
> found in certain neurotic states, when we
> can never remember whether we bolted
> the door; the fiftieth attempt is as uncer-
> tain as the first, as if we could carry out
> the action any number of times without
> its ever giving us the clear, liberating
> memory of having performed it.[17]

This was a fair subjective description
of what we now know as obsessive-

compulsive disorder: a loss of confidence in one's memory, which in its worst cases becomes an inescapable loop. Howard Hughes, the most famous obsessive-compulsive of the twentieth century, would concentrate so intently on regis-tering within his *own* memory what he was saying that he would not realise he was repeating it dozens of times to his con-fused listener.[18] Those poor unfortunates who keep washing their hands or smooth-ing their bed are engaged in a fight with the immediate past, seeking the fixity that will 'confront victoriously' their mercurial forgetfulness.

Wasn't this what had happened between me and Sandra, and the others? Didn't I keep thinking about them, in an autonomic way, purely because *I couldn't remember them*? In stewing on them over and over, I was trying to compensate in quantity of impressions what I lacked in quality. Because I didn't allow, or couldn't entice, any of these girls to make a firm impression on my memory from the outside, I might have been hoping that thousands of imprints of my own imagination would amount to the same thing.

And yet I didn't feel the germs of an obsessive-compulsive disorder in myself. OK, my reading habits had developed some tics. For instance, I would not (and still don't) let myself stop on a palindromic page number. If I am dog-earing the pages, I won't even dog-ear the reverse side of a palindromic page. If I'm bookmarking,

I won't let the bookmark touch the palin-dromic page. So, for instance, if I'm on the train and the stop comes when I'm up to page 121 or 171 or 262 or 656, I will get off and keep reading on the platform until I'm up to 123, say, if I'm dog-earing, or 124 if I'm bookmarking. In every book, when I get to pages 99 through 101, I am in a lather of calculation to avoid stopping on pages 98, 100 and 102, as well as, of course, the dreaded 99 and 101. And a 'nelson'—page 111 and its multiples, 222, 333 and so on—puts me in such a state that if I am reading on an aircraft I believe quite genu-inely that if I'm up to a nelson page when the plane is landing, it will crash. This all sounds crazy, yes, but you'd be surprised how often when I have been forced to stop on a palindromic page number some kind of misfortune has befallen me. I also don't like stopping on page 13.

Still, while increasingly aware of the fragility of my own memory and the power of such superstitions, I didn't sense that I was suffering the beginnings of a disorder. (But if I was, would I be aware of it?) By the 1990s it had become commonplace to interpret many actions as mild manifestations on a spectrum of abnormality— or, looked at another way, to reinterpret mental illnesses as extreme extensions on the plane of normality.[19] My palindrome-phobia was just a mild form of those numerical formulae that completely paralyse some individuals. As a child, on family driving trips I used to make sure my mouth

opened and closed between every drive-
way and cross street we passed. At the
same age, Howard Hughes would count
the telegraph poles between origin and
destination. Many children go through a
phase of avoiding cracks in a footpath.

The medicalisation of human eccentricity can also reshape memory itself. It
has just come back to me how preoccupied
Roy was with cleanliness. He washed his
hands, thoroughly and at length, every
time he came inside the house as well as
before meals—probably fifteen to twenty
times a day. Sharing drinks or cutlery,
and kissing on the lips, were prohibited.
Anyone with a cold was quarantined. He
and Gran travelled a lot, but always with
a bottle of Dettol to wipe down toilet

seats and tap handles in motels or public bathrooms. When my nose remembers Roy, it smells soap. Adopting these habits ourselves, our family accepted them as normal. But the obsessive concern with germs now connotes OCD, and my memories of my grandfather are tilted slightly further off centre.

For some of my twenties I was in a self-diagnostic terror. When we are young adults, not only are we looking for signposts but we are afraid of ourselves, frightened of where our tendencies may lead. Which of my fixations were normal phases, and which were the precursors of a debilitating illness? Are we all just a tiny bit mad, and were my obsessions, like my grandfather's, always going to take on a mild and manageable aspect? Or was I turning into a nasty, obsessive stalker? Were the tics, infatuations, inherited moods and track record of open-ended 'interests' all lining up to shunt me out towards the end of the spectrum, the ultraviolet of normality? I don't think, at that age, I was seriously worried about losing my mind. I was far more preoccupied by the prospect of never being able to enjoy love, and quite afraid of what, unenjoyed, my need for love might turn itself into.

I knew I could suffer abundantly from love—but enjoy it, no. 'Since I loved her,' Proust writes of Gilberte, 'I could only ever see her through the confused desire for more of her, which when you are with the person you love, deprives you of the feeling of loving'.[20] Love was anguish; love was self-defeating; love, if it was true, led only to pain. Up to then, I was concerned only with my own pain. My fixations, like my reading project, were now of an identifiably Proustian nature. I had picked a task without any borders or limits: to know a person fully, to know what she did with every minute of her day, to be known by her, to be immersed fully in each other. An impossible kind of knowledge, in Proust's language it was called 'possession'—the futility of Swann's desire to 'possess' Odette is what drives him mad. I wanted to possess, and to be possessed, in the most nineteenth-century way, but unfortunately my crushes were twentieth-century women. When I started to get worked up, my Gilberte Swann told me to 'chill out'. My Albertine swore like a sailor and married a guy for Austudy. I wanted and hated her so much, could stand so little of her company, that she filled me with an urge to slam the door of whatever room we were in, either to lock her out or lock her in. That one gave me my first presentiment of shifting my pain onto another, as Saint-Loup had sensed about Rachel: 'He was exclusively preoccupied and concerned with what affected her. Through her he was capable of suffering, of being happy, perhaps of killing'.[21]

Was I capable of violence? I didn't think so, but at twenty-four I didn't know who I was yet, and what I did know I didn't want to let out. The kind of love I felt could only be private. Nobody suspected the infatuations I had, because nobody would have thought them possible, not understanding how an obsession links us not to a person but to a thing. And if the object of the infatuation is mistaken for a thing, where will our empathy come from, what will stop us from treating the object of our love as a thing without feelings? If she is just a projection of our desires, what happens when we act, out of frustration and unhappiness, to cauterise those desires? What will stop us from mistaking self-harm for harming someone else? Proust's revelation, which still rang as sonorously for me in my desperate mid-twenties as it had four years earlier, is that obsessive love is an attunement to a song that only we can hear, a racing of our pulse and a sweat in the palms of our hands, a dream we share only with ourselves, and an attachment not to a person but to a deeper part of our own nature. It is a dream, a dangerous involution, and if I had any survival reflex or residual commonsense I would snap out of it.

VI

How do we know when to stop? That's the question Proust always raised for me, and the question he seemed not to be able to answer for himself. The brain-bending length of his literary project ended up killing him. Just as Swann was unable to call a halt to his quest to know everything about Odette, just as all of Proust's central characters, including the narrator himself and the boy-hunting Baron de

Charlus, were unable to find a point at which they said 'Enough', Proust was able to finish his novel cycle only by bringing it to the point at which he started writing it: a perfect circle, revolving inwardly around itself for eternity. He died before the last three volumes were published.

In the intervening years before I read Proust for a third time, I was to meet an obsessive lover who hadn't known when to stop, a projection of my old fears for myself. I was a juror in the case of Malcolm Potier, and wrote a book about it.[22] After his wife left him, Potier had tried three times to have her murdered. He would go on to try another time, and for all I know he is still trying today. He once said, 'I will never ever give up'.

Potier is English, once a high-flying property developer and a titled gent, the laird of the Scottish island of Gigha, which he had bought. When his de facto marriage broke down and he discovered his partner was resuming an old liaison with an Australian boyfriend, Potier came here and tried to hire a hitman to murder the boyfriend. Having failed, Potier was arrested for entering Australia illegally and put into immigration detention. While at Villawood detention centre, he paid an Italian detainee $10 000 to kill both the ex-partner and the boyfriend. The Italian ran off to Italy with Potier's money. Then, through a go-between, Potier arranged a third hitman to kill the pair. This third hitman was an undercover policeman who taped their conversations, and these tapes formed the main evidence in Potier's five-week trial.

I watched Potier every day for a month. He was tall, distinguished by a striking bald dome and a long top lip. He conducted himself with supreme confidence, an intelligent and capable man who was heartbroken and angry but didn't know how to stop. As a juror, my mind was too occupied with the question of 'Did he do it?' to progress to the question of why. But a man's motive to kill the woman he loves is one of those gaps that are surprisingly easy to fill. We know so many of them, these men whose love can speak only in the language of violence. Women, too. Where does love become so overwhelming that it becomes a volatile substance? What is it that makes our most cherished passion— passion itself—lose its regulating facility so that, like cancer, it cannot stop itself from growing? What kind of love has only this one way of letting itself out?

I knew intimately what it felt like. Where does love lead in Proust? To the narrator taking Albertine prisoner, locking her up, as good as murdering her, because that is the only way he can satisfy his desire for possession. I am well aware that there are profound degrees of difference between Malcolm Potier and the lovelorn serial stalker that I was. Crossing the line to violence has many causes. I know now that I am not a man capable of that kind of violence. But I didn't know that when I was twenty, or twenty-four, and it was that unknown that made me so frightened of the strength of feelings which were fed, aided and abetted, by the great literature of the Western world. By the time I met Potier, I could easily look back on my barren youthful entanglements as a normal and cherished rite of passage, but I had not forgotten what it felt like, and in Potier I could see what, in the real world, this kind of love can do when it cannot find its point of exhaustion.

VII

Reading Proust for a third time, I was past forty, a husband and father, and the future was no longer so frightful. The joys of rereading this book after such a long break were manifold. First, I had my own Proust-within-Proust moments: in a flash, a certain paragraph would summon up 1986, sitting on the wooden outdoor furniture near my parents' swimming pool. Another passage

I recalled reading while sitting on a lawn I used to mow as a student. What came alive was not my entire past, but my Proust-past, what Proust called 'a sort of superabundant sweetness and mysterious density'.[23] And I now paid more attention to the footnotes, discovering for instance that the 'Bressant' style of haircut favoured by Swann 'consisted of wearing the hair in a crew-cut in front and longer at the back'.[24] So Charles Swann, belle epoque art expert, the aristocracy's glamorous pet, one of literature's greatest doomed lovers, had a mullet!

In the eighteen years since my second reading, quite a lot had changed for me. I had learnt a few things about love. I had dared to let the lion out of its cage and declare myself to the sufferer of one of my old-fashioned crushes. To my astonishment, it turned into my first true love. It didn't last, but it freed me. At twenty-eight I would meet someone else upon whom I quickly settled my power for infatuation. For a mercifully short time I suffered terrible agonies of wanting to know what she was doing every minute, and sat up all of one night spying on her; I discovered nothing, came into possession of none of that precious knowledge that is the real love-object of the jealous lover, but in the end she trusted me to trust her, and we lived together, married and had children. It was a Goldilocks case of obsessive love: a little bit of heat, but not too much, being just right.

What had changed most of all, however, were my feelings towards Proust—or towards life as seen through the Proustian prism. While the many compressors and popularisers of Proust have bastardised his books into capsules of oracular wisdom, I had moved in the opposite direction.[25] By this stage I had lost my unquestioning reverence. But it was not my critical reading that had changed so much as my personal relationship with his book. While Proust gives any humdrum life the wonderful potentiality to be converted into art, he can fool us (he fooled me) into thinking that every thread of life is interesting if teased out sufficiently, and all truth is found if we go 'downwards, into ourselves'. He fools us (he fooled me) into thinking that

recapitulation, introspection and self-pity,
bleak pessimism and paranoia, are always
the best materials and tools for the creation of art. I had slowly learnt, in the intervening years, that they were not, or were
not for me.

The problem was not Proust so much
as my hero-worshipping young mind when
I first read him. What I have fully grasped
only in my third reading is that the comic
tone in Proust extends far beyond the
caricatures of society people. The author
is laughing at his neurotic narrator and
trusting us to laugh with him. The last
thing Proust intended was for his book to
be taken as seriously as a religious text. As
much as he extols the redemptive powers
of art, he also laughs at it: when the Baron

de Charlus is humiliated in his pursuit of
the nasty young violinist Charles Morel,
the Baron 'merged his own situation
with that described by Balzac, he had in
some sense taken refuge in the novel … '.[26]
Perhaps I was just too earnest to understand Proust's variations in tone.

My uneasy third reading went deeper
than this, beyond the literary. As I read
some passages, I grew confused. There is
a point at which the narrator writes:

> … though I thought of nothing else but
> of not going a single day without seeing
> Gilberte … yet those moments when I
> was with her and which since the day
> before I had been awaiting so impa-
> tiently, for which I had trembled, for

which I would have sacrificed everything else, were in no way happy moments.

He was obsessed with her, but his time with her gave him 'not one atom of pleasure'.[27] Hang on, I thought, this sounds a lot like what happened between me and someone when I was at university, at the time I was first reading Proust. Then there is an episode in which Saint-Loup is tortured by Rachel's silence. '"What have I done to make her keep so silent? Perhaps she hates me, and will go on hating me forever." And he blamed himself for it. So silence was in fact driving him mad, with jealousy and remorse.'[28] But this was *exactly* what I was thinking about someone who had failed to reply to a letter of mine.

Or was it? Could it be that those obsessive loves didn't actually happen to me but to Proust's narrator instead? Was I so immersed in him, so *spoken to* by him, that his experience became a surrogate for mine, to the extent that I coloured in the gaps in my memories with his, or even substituted his for my own? What I have written about Sandra and the others, did that really happen, or is it a broth of life, Proust, my other reading—the great novels, after all, are mostly if not exclusively concerned with unhappy love—and my own attempts to write? Even now, I find that my precious Proust-within-Proust moments were anticipated by him. A book, he wrote, may 'turn into something immaterial, akin to all the preoccupations or sensations we have at that particular time, and mingle indissolubly with them. Some name, read long ago in a book, contains among its syllables the strong wind and bright sunlight of the day when we were reading it'.[29] But wasn't that what I was just saying? So when I felt this echo of the swimming pool or the lawn I mowed, was I remembering an actual experience or just a line I had read?

I don't know the answers, and my memory is becoming shaky enough to raise a few questions. Just recently, I met someone who had been a mutual friend of mine and the Albertine about whom I felt so dangerously passionate many years ago. I remember, around the time my obsession had worn off (to find itself a new host), how offended I was when the mutual friend made the passing comment that she felt sorry for me 'because you have such a huge crush' on Albertine. Outrage ripped me in opposing directions. This was no mere 'crush'; this was a buzz-saw of longing!—but also, it was over by then, so how terribly unfair that it had become public knowledge. I was furious. But more than twenty years later, when I met that mutual friend again, she said: 'So did you know Albertine?' Not only had she forgotten the insult, she had forgotten the crush, and she might as well have forgotten me.

It could be that I am chasing shadows, that what I search for in my grandfather and father may exist neither in them nor in me, and the uncertainty and anxiety I once felt over what I might become has given way to an uncertainty, now, in memory, over what I was.

I suspect, at the very least, that Proust's influence on me was to glorify the worst of my self-pity, to kid me into believing that art must involve a certain kind of suffering, even invite and create that suffering, in order then to redeem it. So I cherished and brought upon myself a state of mind that was somehow false, the tail wagging the dog. There are essential aspects of being a Parisian living from 1871 to 1923 that cannot be shared by an Australian born in 1966, not least the matrix of cultural references, both classical and topically French, that underlies the text of *In Search of*

Lost Time. The illusion that a writer knows us, speaks to our heart, is the most powerful magic trick that literature can pull, but as a young man living through the page I had forgotten that it was, after all, an illusion. Discovering the universality of human experience is all very well, but taken in too high a dose it can be as alienating and untrue as the opposite, the worship of our particularity.

I took pride in my obsessiveness without honestly asking whether this was me or someone inhabiting me. But I am not Proust's narrator any more than I am Don Quixote or Captain Ahab. Mistaking myself for them was the most harmful effect of my grand reading project. I was unsure, for many years, whether I was afraid of being sick with my obsessions, or hoped that I was. Now I might have to resign myself to being happy, healthy, more normal than I suspected, and not quite so driven. I am still on the grand reading project, but the difference now is that I entertain no delusions of finishing it, and because it can't be finished it has no end towards which it is progressing; and because it has no direction, happily for me it can no longer be called a project.

Meanwhile, in the eighteen years since my second reading of Proust the Western world's knowledge of obsessions and manias had become, well, almost an obsession. Alcoholism had been joined by the newly medicalised workaholism, sexaholism and shopaholism. We had long known of kleptomania and pyromania, but now we were familiar with trichotillomania (obsessive pulling out of hair) and the many and growing obsessive body dismorphic disorders. Our popular culture had taken to its bosom the plastic surgery addict, the tattoo addict, the porn addict, the obsessive gamer, the Elvis lookalike, the conspiracy-theory nutter and the collector of Pez dispensers. We knew about the woman who embezzled thousands of dollars to buy Barbie dolls.[30] It was easy to forget that when I'd last read Proust there was no such thing as the internet; by now, the internet had not only given every obsessive person a home and a community but had spawned its own meta-obsession, the obsession with being on the internet.

Meanwhile, I had moved in the opposite direction. It might be an act of kindness towards the mentally ill that we see their problems as continuous with our own foibles, so that they are not 'other'. But at the same time it invites the kind of intellectual slackness where we forget that between me and my wild-eyed letters, between being jealous of Albertine and locking her up, between Malcolm Potier being angry with his ex-wife and trying to have her murdered, there are differences, and sometimes these differences are more important than the similarities.

For me, Proust gave a push to certain indulgences which needed no help. In his world, obsessiveness redeems everything. In our world, obsessiveness is the sine qua non for success. 'History belongs', as Peter van Onselen and Wayne Errington paraphrase the quintessential suburban politician John Howard's credo, 'to those who turn up'.[31] The main requirement for great personal success is indistinguishable from a diagnosis of what in Proust's time was called mania and in ours is often called bipolar disorder. As we have become more conscious of the tricks marketers play on our psyche, moreover, we could make the obvious point that if they could turn our desires for products into obsessions, that would be consumer culture's apotheosis. And then, beyond that, it's also perhaps too self-evident to mention that we live in the time of a war which is open-ended and eternal—as soon as we entered it we were too far in to turn around. The dilemma of the War on Terror reminds me of nothing so much as my idea that I could read everything.

What I saw as a quest for purity was, in retrospect, a retreat from life. If I could bury myself in a lifelong quest then I could avoid a lot of inconvenient questions. The quest promised to take care of my days for me, relieve me of wondering what to do. If I could immerse my romantic life in a poetry of suffering, I could glorify, through literature, my basic cowardice. It's not beyond question that my infatuations were of the type La Bruyere described (quoted approvingly by Proust): 'Men often want to love where they cannot succeed, they seek their defeat without being able to bring it about and so, if I may put it like this, they are compelled to remain free'.[32]

So much twaddle is said about the limitless benefits of consuming books, as if they were leafy green vegetables. My experience is that reading is, while a superior part of life, a part of life nonetheless, subject to the same dangers as anything else. For someone such as I, who placed literature on a pedestal above all else and tended to press infatuations a little too far, to have my tendencies valorised by the great novels as noble and heroic was confusing and corrupting, and I do believe that instead of floating out of my depth with Proust and our phantoms I should have talked with and listened to more real live girls.

Roy died in 1995; in 2000 and 2004 my father suffered two strokes. For all the medical diagnoses and prognoses and other mumbo jumbo, those of us who know him know one thing for certain: the main cause of his strokes was his own personality, which has nearly killed him, twice, and that gives us all pause for thought.

In 2002 and 2003 I became a father. For all the talk of 'obsessive' and 'addictive' personalities, it is not the case that the person who is obsessive about some things is obsessive about everything. I have never, for example, been an obsessive parent. I can see the temptation of becoming single-minded about raising children, for they offer the ultimate temptation for total control, sucking parents into a dual vacuum of possibility (I can make their life perfect!) and danger (I can protect them from everything!). It has differences from obsessive romantic love—even the most obsessive parents don't scratch their kids' names into the walls and stare dreamily out of windows imagining what they are doing—but it invites the same will to *possess*. In any case, for whatever reasons, and I can thank my own parents for this, obsessive parenting hasn't been my bag.

However, I can see the clarity of the bloodline in my six-year-old son. Every night, he cannot be at peace until he has seen the ABC news weather forecast. Since his infancy, he has had a peculiar fixation with watching the forecast and repeating its details aloud. From one viewing he can memorise a five-day forecast, and is always pleased to report that tomorrow will be sunny, rainy or windy. I never knew a six-year-old could be so fascinated by weather, but I know where it comes from. (Proust: 'Was it not enough that I should bear an exaggerated resemblance to my father, not just consulting the barometer as he did but becoming a kind of human barometer myself … ')[33]

There have been nights when we have asked him to come to dinner rather than watch the weather. Dinner is on the table, and cannot wait. Normally a peaceful boy, he once flew into a temper I'd never seen, in him at least. The weather would not wait until after dinner! He had lost sight of the possibility that time would continue after dinner (and that we have the Weather Channel). The weather had to be watched now, and he was prepared to tear down the house to watch it.

I had seen this before, not in him but in three generations of his DNA.

How do we know when to stop? For the males in my family, I'm not sure that it is something we can know, even less exercise a choice over. Not knowing when to stop is just one of those things, like baldness and big noses, that we're saddled with, and the best we can hope is to grow into proportion with it. I often think it is only a concatenation of luck and instinct and the wiser heads of those who are not of a one-track mind (my son's mother, his sister, his grandmothers) that will steer him away from trouble. I have little doubt that he will one day be one of those lovers who hum to themselves the mantra of their beloved's name and burn with anxiety over what that person is doing at any given moment. His sister might be that type too. If this is the kind of lover they become, then at least they should know whom to blame.

What is clearest to me, when I see my son lose himself in his grand passions, is that single-mindedness is our kind of trance. It is our vacation. When we are lost in our dream, our time is accounted for, we have no questions to ask ourselves, we are on a holiday in our own company, hidden in plain view. The one-track mind is our fortress, our safety zone. It defies logic, it is not defensible and it is often destructive.

It will make of our lives a series of grand projects, many unfinishable. It is the most pointless thing, and all the more seductive for its pointlessness. But here's what I wish I knew and would like to tell him: it is not something of which he should be either too proud, or too afraid.

Notes

1 Les Carlyon, *The Great War*, Macmillan, Sydney, 2006, p. 552: 'He wrote in his tiny diary: "Met Dad at WC Club at night while air raid on London." This was a long essay for Howard. His diary, smaller than his hand, is a series of laconic entries and understatements: "Inoculated again", "First day in trenches", "Shoved in old barn". When his best friend was killed he would write: "Will wounded and dies."'.

2 Pat Barker, *Regeneration*, Penguin, London, 1992, p. 114.

3 David Wallechinsky, Irving Wallace, Amy Wallace and Sylvia Wallace, *The Book of Lists*, Corgi, London, 1978.

4   Marcel Proust, *In Search of Lost Time*, vol. 2,
    ed. Christopher Prendergast, Penguin, London,
    2002, p. 413. In 1986 and 1990 I read the Kilmar-
    tin translation, titled *Remembrance of Things Past*,
    but page references in this essay are to the 2002
    translation, *In Search of Lost Time*.

5   Vladimir Nabokov, *Lolita*, Penguin, London, 1980,
    p. 40: ' ... my knees were like reflections of knees
    in rippling water, and my lips were like sand ... '.

6   Proust, vol. 2, p. 42.

7   ibid., vol. 2, p. 437.

8   ibid., vol. 1, p. 345.

9   ibid., vol. 4, p. 261.

10 ibid., vol. 5, p. 68: 'Was it not enough that I should
    bear an exaggerated resemblance to my father, not
    just consulting the barometer as he did but becom-
    ing a kind of human barometer myself ... Once we
    pass a certain age, the soul of the child we used
    to be and the souls of the dead from whom we
    spring come and scatter over us handfuls of their
    riches and their misfortunes, asking to bear a part
    in the new feelings we are experiencing: feelings
    which allow us, rubbing out their old effigies, to
    recast them in an original creation. Thus, all my
    past since my earliest years, and beyond those,

my relatives' past, mixed into my carnal love for
Albertine the sweetness of a love both filial and
maternal. Once a certain hour has come we have to
welcome them, all those relatives who have come
so far to assemble around us.'

11 Alan Bennett, *The Uncommon Reader*, Faber &
Faber/Profile, London, 2007.

12 Proust, vol. 2, p. 484.

13 ibid., vol. 1, p. 311.

14 The DSM is known for its current version, which
since 1994 has been DSM-IV. DSM-V will be
published in draft version in 2009.

15 Jorge Luis Borges, quoted in *Harper's*, April 2008:
at 85, 'if I think about my past life, I think of
course about friends, lovers also, but I think most
of all about books'.

16 Proust, vol. 1, p. 27.

17 ibid., vol. 5, p. 52.

18 Luke Davies, *The God of Speed*, Allen & Unwin,
Sydney, 2008.

19 This resulted in a boom in self-reporting. The
believed incidence of OCD in the last ten years
has risen from one in 500 people to one in 50.

20 Proust, vol. 2, p. 104.

21 ibid., vol. 3, p. 153.

22 Malcolm Knox, *Secrets of the Jury Room*, Random
    House, Sydney, 2005. I met Potier in Silverwater
    jail in late 2001. He had just been convicted. In
    the book I wrote I was not allowed to identify him
    personally, as his appeal process and the second
    trial were incomplete. I can identify him now.

23 Proust, vol. 1, p. 302.

24 ibid., vol. 1, note 2 to chapter 1.

25 There is no way Proust, or any other fiction,
    should be read as a handbook to life, and yet by the
    time I read Proust for a third time he had become
    a cliché, compressed and manufactured into an
    industry of fey little primers for the time-poor.
    Like many readers of Proust who claim a certain
    possessiveness (I think of the Gary Larson cartoon
    of the dismayed fans of a garage band gone big-
    time—'We knew them before they were good!'),
    I detest books like Alain de Botton's *How Proust
    Can Change Your Life*, the condensing of the great
    fictive dream into life lessons. A friend of mine, a
    PhD in Proust, calls him 'Alain de Bottom of de
    Barrel'. I have no sense of humour or tolerance
    towards this kind of book, which, to paraphrase
    an infinitely smarter English writer, Geoff Dyer,
    might be retitled *Proust for People Who Can't Be*

Bothered Reading Him. How can Proust change
your life? Try reading him, for a start.

26 Proust, vol. 4, p. 452.

27 ibid., vol. 1, p. 403.

28 ibid., vol. 3, p. 119.

29 ibid., vol. 6, p. 193.

30 Rosemary Heinen, featured in a BBC television
series called *Obsessions*, embezzled money to buy
among other things 600 Barbie dolls.

31 Peter van Onselen and Wayne Errington, *John
Winston Howard: The Biography*, Melbourne
University Press, Melbourne, 2007.

32 Quoted in Proust, vol. 6, p. 203.

33 Proust, vol. 5, p. 68.

Malcolm Knox is the author of three internationally published novels—*Summerland*, *A Private Man* and *Jamaica*—as well as several works of nonfiction. His journalism has won two Walkley Awards and a Human Rights Award, and he has been a runner-up in the Graham Perkin Award for Australian Journalist of the Year. He lives in Sydney.